BEAST MODE @ INDIAN STOCK MARKET

THE BIGGER SHORT 2025

DR. RAVI N HUMBARWADI

Contents

Foreword

The Solitaire Millionaire

At the mid and depth of the recession lies the greatest opportunity to become a millionaire. At this point of greatest sense of loss lie fantastic companies at rock bottom bargain valuations. That is when you should deploy the cash which you would have if you sold off the rise.

The fastest rate of millionaires was post the Great Depression 1929. Crashes and recessions are the best opportunities for a canny investor to become a millionaire.

Preface

This Time The Bear Will Eat Robin Hoods For Breakfast
What About Lunch $ Dinner. Read to Find Out

Prologue

The year of Crashes, Corrections and Dips : 2025.

There is only one guaranteed sector plus one more sector which you can buy on the way down. Defence and Renewable . Geopolitical uncertainty, Europe and USA disconnect leading to increased military demand from Europe and spectre of war in middle east, China - Taiwan, India borders on all sides and jet fighter and submarine deficiency in India make defence a compelling buy on dips and crashes. Read to find out which possible dates to enter the sector.

Trump is blind to climate change. but climate change is real and nature will take revenge of human excesses sooner than later. That's when renewables will come back as screaming buys. Read to know more about Indian stock market.

ONE

GEOPOLITICS

The brew just got what it didn't need. As if the US economy and Trump tariffs were not enough to invite the bear in, geopolitics will impact the markets too. And how!

Zelensky was not invited by Trump for his Swearing In. Ukraine is done and dusted even before Trump takes charge? Not so easy babae. It's not that simple. NATO members may choose to follow Trump. Some may not. But I always thought that NATO had outlived its utility even by 2000. You know what happens when you get expired medicine – its poison. Russia was nicely integrated into the world. It didn't trouble anyone. And it had only 1 demand. Let NATO not come to its large border with Ukraine. There was no need actually. And If Ukraine did want a sense of security it should have got itself integrated with European Union or rest of the world business or otherwise. Russia would not have laid a finger on it other than verbal volleys sometimes.

Was it the American arms lobby that wanted to get fat or the moronic policy makers with dementia who equated Russia as an enemy for all time without being aware we had moved ahead. It was the American mindset that got us an European war rather than reality. Anyways this is what Trump thinks. Being a businessman at heart knowing the perilous US economic condition he wants to save money for USA to MAGA! So no more money to the war. That's good for the market. If it happens.

So anyways, that's a big positive if and when it happens. When the market gets a whiff of the end of the Russo-Ukraine war via Trump, it's a reward that can spike the market to some highs.

However 2025 is all about booking profits when you see them. Coz I can guarantee you one thing this year; dips, corrections, crashes more than once.

A few times actually. So you are ready to buy those 15 day crashes and 1 month substantial corrections. And of course I have the dates in this book that will let you know exactly when such events are likely to happen. This way you can actually sit on neat profits and even double your investment this year when others are crying their way to wherever.

But for this you need to have a sense of the time when this will happen. I am not saying time the market.

I am only saying when you see green in your portfolio please take the money that is being offered to you. Please. But if you do want to time the markets then this book is for you. As I said I have the likely time mapped out in this book.

And sit back for the big dip and crash. Round the corner.

If you don't have your nose in the air or ear to the ground "Don't worry the noise of this will reach you." Coz the correction will be big. And wait and buy in sip mode when it happens. These dips will go down and down and down. So the Sip mode.

The other fast track method is to buy shorts. Become the Big Short of 2025! And get a movie made in your name. This is the year Boss, for being a bear.

I would say there's more money to be made in 2025 by shorting. But shorting is an art that needs a heart and a skill that is rare.

TWO

BIG BEAR INVITES OF 2025

One after another there are bear invites coming - To join The Big Bear Parties of 2025. The First Invite is from The US Economy.

1. **US Economy**

37 Trillion dollar debt. Debt to GDP ratio: 125 %.

No wonder, Trump is in a hurry to save US money wherever he can. Including the dollar guzzling Ukraine war. Biden was not bothered. Dementia?

It is now at a level seen during major conflicts (the US debt) – think WW2. Ominous.

"On the road to bankruptcy." I am not saying that. Elon Musk a government guy did. Every US citizen has a debt of $1,08,000. Some of them are conveniently blaming Covid.

And geopolitics is just going to get heated up (Middle East and China - Taiwan). The defence spending is only going to get worse. Oil price will go down due to recession fears. However once Middle East heats up oi price will do no favor. Inflation will make a U turn and make the Fed go crazy and Trump as well.

These above few lines if you understand will make you dump stocks and rush towards gold.

US has printed money without a gold backup (historically removed by Nixon). That has indeed let to print at will syndrome that will surely catch up once the unemployment numbers start rising (keep an eye on the unemployment rate).

Net interest payment now makes up 13 % of spending! As much as defence and health care just below Social security and Medicare. Home, Car and Health insurance have shot up. Home insurance doesn't cover earthquake insurance. You need to get a separate policy. Mangione happened for a reason. The drift is, it's all so costly. Nothi' ain't cheap or reasonable anymore.

Debt can be reduced by spending cuts (reason for Trump withdrawal of funds for Ukraine and other useless grants).

Keep a keen eye on unemployment. The government itself will begin the layoffs.

The holders of US treasury Bonds are various countries around the world. Any stress on these bonds can send shock waves thru the world markets. To continue to roll over the debt on these bonds USA has to pay more due to the sharp increase in interest rate due to the high rate environment existing now.

At current rates, the U.S. national debt is growing by a remarkable $1 trillion about every 100 days

Interest payment itself is 1 trillion dollars. It makes you squirm if you are human and a citizen of USA.

A debt trap. A debt spiral. But maybe Trump can pull it off. With help from tech support DOGE. But not before a lot of economic pain in 2025. I wrote this before Trump himself said this today.

2. **The Rise of Gold and Silver**

Dollar gains strength Rupee weakens. FII outflows from India. Inflation rises in the West. The middle-east will heat up time to time and oil trends up. Rate cuts are not as many as people would like. Stocks crash from time to time. These are interconnected and intricate and ultimately pummel the stocks. So due to such multiple issues people rush to safety. So more pain for stocks due to money outflow and competition from other asset classes.

Gold and Silver rise.

Real Estate. Expect some jhatkas in the year of wild swings.

There will be bouts of extreme panic. But since India as a country is the world's topmost growth story there will be pullbacks and spikes now and then in 2025. But again I repeat the pull-back will be more in sectors such as defence and power including renewables. Banks and real estate will be pummeled. This statement will be repeated in this book - 2025 is the year of crashes, corrections and dips.

3. **Buffet Sitting on Record Cash.**

I can see something you still can't dumbos.

Buffet: Buffet is selling more and more. He holds more cash as a percentage than before the 2008 crash. Buffet has sold 2/3 of Apple shares he held. He's selling Bank of America regularly.

Buffett's company sold roughly 600 million shares of Apple. Buffet has sold 25 % of his Bank of America holding. Wells Fargo JP Morgan Goldman Sachs. Can you imagine how much of these Buffet has sold. 100%. Yes 100% of these bank stocks. His holding is zilch in these banks.

Berkshire's cash on hand grew to $325.2 billion at the end of the third quarter, up from roughly $276.9 billion at the end of the second quarter. Cash at all time record high.

"But I don't mind at all, under current conditions, building the cash position. I think when I look at the alternative of what's available in the equity markets, and I look at the composition of what's going on in the world, we find it quite attractive."

We are all dodos if we still can't read between the lines or see the light filtering between the curtain lines.

Please read it again and again. All it means is: Keep cash. I can see something you still can't dumbos.

In India SBI has shown great profit. But its margins are not great. And cascading effect of the Western economy woes having a cascading effect of emerging countries will make banks a pathetic story through 2025. Real estate in India will show the effect of high base and post Covid continued consumption of 3 years. The dip and correction could turn into a real estate crash post mid May 2025.

4. **The Yield Curve: The Greatest Ever Predictor.**

-1.88. This is the largest it has inverted in the last 5 decades!

6 to 18 months from the inversion you get a recession. The 18 month is done. So where's the recession? Just round the corner.

10 Y- # M curve Uninverted in Dec 2024 after 780 days of inversion.

Uninversion:

0.1 pc - 1989

0.5 pc - 2001

1 pc - 2007

In 2007 uninversion happened to the extent of 1 pc and in 2008 there was the big crash. From 2007 we can infer a 3 month gap between a recession and the uninversion.

You can see above that in other prior years, the uninversion of the yield curve have been followed by historical crashes.

Uninversion has happened now in December 2024. I would keep the one of market crash to peak in March end – April 2025.

5. Unemployment

If it's anything that will break the S/P or Dow Jones it will be the uptick in unemployment rates.

The US unemployment had inched up to 4.2 %. Last year it was 3.7 %. The long term average is 5.6 %. Keep a keen eye on these numbers. This starts creeping up from 4.2 % then you are staring at the writing on the wall. If the unemployment rate trends up then it confirms one more nail, possibly the final nail in Dow Jones. DOGE has already made a beginning. These stats will start showing up. And then all hell will break loose.

There is nothing like no jobs to hit the investors who have been on a joy ride till now. For Robin Hoods this will be a first time experience of the bear. And it can be sickening. Belive me I have experience it.

THREE

THE GRAPHS SAY IT ALL

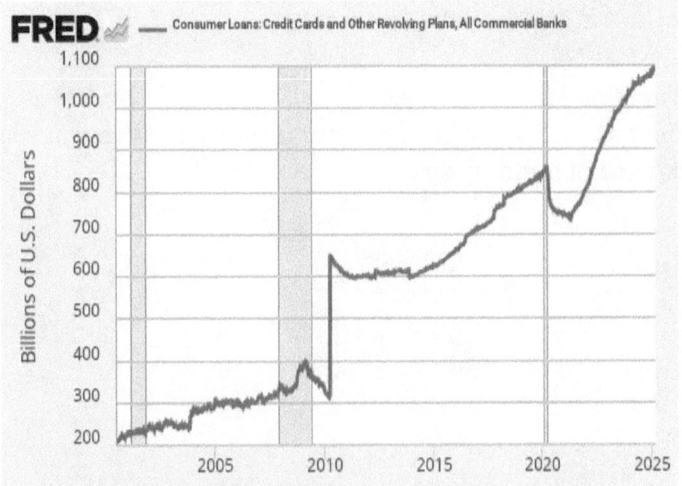

Source: Board of Governors of the Federal Reserve System (US) via FRED®
Shaded areas indicate U.S. recessions.

Consumer Loan and Credit Cards: All Time High.

If there is delinquency then it's a steep fall from there. No wonder Buffet has emptied his tank of banks.

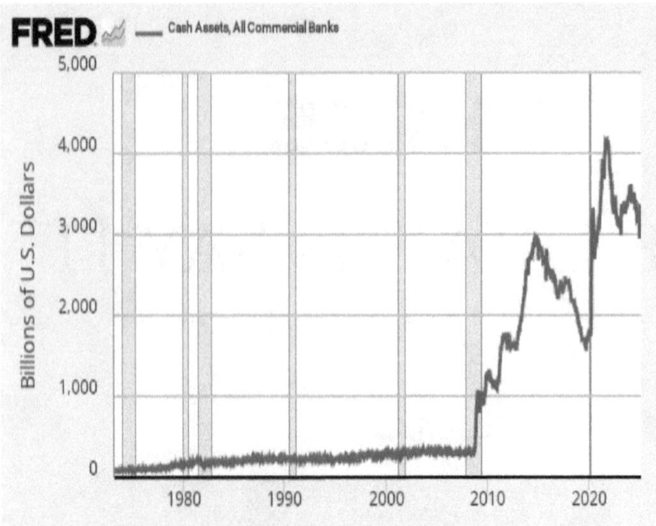

Source: Board of Governors of the Federal Reserve System (US) via FRED®
Shaded areas indicate U.S. recessions.

Bear territory from End Mar - Apr: 2025.

Consumer credit is at All Time high (previous graph). Here you can see the cash assets of banks are trending down.

FOUR
ASTRO ANGLE

Mercury Combust: Fluctuations Guaranteed.

Let's take an example : 21 Jan - 22 Feb - See what happened during this period of Mercury Combust

27 Jan to 4 Feb: 1000 point up in Budget Expectations. Then 1300 point down till 18 Feb: Trump Tariffs. Stocks crumbled. Nifty down. Spikes were sold into. It was Sell on Rise period.

Rest of the period till 22 Feb was down with minor spikes.

Conclusion: The spikes get sold into during a Mercury combust period and the stocks are beaten down a lot.

The coming similar Mercury Combust Periods in 2025.

17 Mar - 4 Apr

18 May - 8 Jun

19-Jul - 11 Aug

3 Sep - 4 Oct

13 Nov -27 Nov

Mercury Combust plus retrograde (Vakri): <u>Very Big Fluctuations</u>

17 Mar-4 Apr

19 Jul-11 Aug

13 Nov- 27 Nov

Both side movements are expected. But when macro situation is bad then it is more of a big downfall. Sell on Rise kind of scenario. Big Falls.

Possible Bad Period for stocks

20 Mar- 12 Apr

4th Sep - 5th Oct

I am not an astro expert. But I have collated the information that could provide some dates for the bearish scenario that we are all expecting to happen. This can be a added aid for for experts and HNI's who can handle futures and options.

<u>Other Events as per Astro</u>

Mar last week to Apr first two weeks: Water related disaster.

In 2025

Gold is Up. Will touch or even cross Rs. 1 lakh.

Oil will go up later when middle-east tension starts. Inflation will be more.

FII/FDI outflow continues. Real Estate fluctuations and crash May 2nd week onwards

Gold could provide a dip and opportunity to buy in the last week of Feb to first week of Mar. After which it is one way ticket to the Moon. 19 Mar could be the start of big move in gold.

Mar 17 /22/29 to Apr 14 2025: Market fall accelerates. I would sell on dead cat bounces in between during this time period. The fluctuations can be big and crazy.

Mar-19 – Mar 24 and Mar 29 onwards could see bigger falls.

Gold-Silver: Any dips between 25 Feb to 4 Mar 2025 I would buy in SIP mode. If people have not entered already when it was 75K. This window period could provide an opportunity to climb a running train.

India could see action around Chicken Neck or in North – North East in Mid- year or post mid-year.

4 Sep - 4 Oct 2025 could be another big fall in the stock market.

Basically banks are a goner this year I believe which already has happened to some extent in Jan – Feb. Real Estate post mid-year, after mid-May could see huge fall.

Gold will touch 1 lack rupees sooner than you think. Mid May there could a cooling off of gold. Gold is on a run. Blue sky.

Mar 22 2025: The coming 9 months the morning star Venus portends unrest or war in the world.

Fluctuations in stock market, real estate in 2025. Falls are prominent. 2025 is the year of falls, dips and crashes with up-spikes and dead cat bounces in between.

FIVE

BECOME THE GREEN ALIEN

Apollo Micro Systems.

The stock gave of 825 per cent in 3 years and 1,600 per cent in 5 years.

Apollo Micro Systems born in 1985 is a in the business of creating, constructing, and validating electronics and electro-mechanical solutions for aerospace, defence, and space. torpedo-homing systems and underwater mines. The latest results in Jan 2025 saw its sales increase by 62.5 per cent to Rs 148 crore and profit after tax (PAT) increased by 83.1 per cent to Rs 18.24 crore in Q3FY25

Apollo Micro Systems Limited (AMS) and Garden Reach Shipbuilders & Engineers (GRSE) have partnered in a 5-year MoU to develop and export advanced weapon and electronic systems, focusing on underwater and air defence technologies for both defence and commercial sectors. This collaboration is in addition to developing new systems will also offer modernization services.

This happened after Redon Systems Pvt Ltd and Apollo Micro Systems Limited signed a Consortium Agreement to work together on a manufacturing relationship. They intend to acquire Automatic Landing Module systems and work jointly to build solutions for Allied systems and Loitering Munition.

The above two news modules shows the hunger, agility and recognition of the new hero in the town by other biggies. I like the back to back news. And I like Apollo micro systems. My favorite stock of 2025-26

Custom Built Electronic Hardware & Software solutions for Mission Critical applications. State-of-the-art technologies for the Aerospace,

Defence, Space, Transportation and Home Land Security markets. AMS is a service provider and R & D partner for BEL. Its client list includes HAL, BHEL, ONGC, NTPC and other biggies. Which means AMS is not only into defence but homeland security as well.

In Jan 2025, **Apollo Micro Systems** raised Rs. 381 crores through preferential issue at   ₹114 per share. Expansion of facility is on. And the base strong support is Rs.102 for you – PE in mid 20's. There you have it. Very attractive rate for an exponentially growing company. I just can't have enough of AMS.

Apollo Micro Systems Ltd. aims to double its revenues in FY26 amid anticipation of some "very big ticket" projects. The company's current order book stands at about Rs 550-570 crore. Each of the expected projects can be more than the company's revenues of the last three years put together and much more than that in a single order—Rs 1,000 crore - Rs 1,500 crore and above. The company can achieve 100% revenue growth the coming year.

AMS has partnered with DRDO in several of the indigenous missile programs and are part of 60% of the technologies. Many of these programs are entering into the production phase in the next few months and years. Therefore, the 45-50% revenue growth will continue to happen for at least three more years. This information was provided by the management.

AMS is my favorite stock. I am buying this.

Watch Out: But keep an eye whether all these orders do come in. Coz entire bullishness is based on the order inflow.

Highlights

Capacity Expansion to 4.5 Lac sq feet from 50K sq ft: Next few months. Rapid. Too much!

Dec 31 2025: Expected order book: 2500 cr- 3000 cr on a conservative estimate.

Some more just AMS things: Rockets - guided and unguided, 100 m to 400 m depth for mines for the navy. Man portable mines. The list keeps expanding.

I saw the 5 year graph and was surprised to see this trading at a low of Rs 3. Now at Rs 106 it is again as a symbolic Rs 3. I can see the new capacity kicking in, the new big orders flowing in the next few months and the extension of its skills and capacities, its recognition by other industry majors and forays in all 3 arms of the military - the navy, airforce and army. A 4 figure 1000 is on the cards. A ten bagger in 2 years for me – AMS.

Year High: Rs. 157

Price Today: Rs. 106 (After the Jan Result: Lucky me)

With PE now about 28 and recent PE around 80 plus, this is a great buy for me now. And I will add more if it dips below. I want to hold a minimum of 1 year and take it up from there depending on project updates.

Bharat Electronics

"This one needs no intro. Rugged old warhorse with a new spring in its activities BEL is one cocky defence player that knows where it stands and where it is heading. With over 80,000 crores in its kitty a mega order of 25,000 cr of QRSAM a possibility and even otherwise from EASE radars to all things electronics, it's is a stable, dividend paying, low risk high return guaranteed stock. One a kind in these unpredictable times with multiple downgrades across sectors this is one stock I will buy on every dip and buy even more in a market crash. Need I Say more?

Price I would buy: Rs 240

HAL

It is at the moment of weakness when the greatest profits can be made. With the engine problems haunting it since he few months this holds true for the India monopoly behemoth HAL.

The defence ministry has issued a tender to Bengaluru-based plane maker Hindustan Aeronautics Limited (HAL) for the proposed acquisition of 156 Prachand light combat helicopters (LCH)

The new helicopters, 90 for the army and 66 for IAF, are estimated to cost ₹50,000 crore. The RFP has already been released months back. Once the order for 156 helicopters is signed, HAL will execute the order in about six years.

There is another order for 97 light combat aircraft (LCA Mk-1A) at a time of acute shortage of fighter squadrons worth   ₹67,000 crore.

HAL has thus far manufactured 15 limited series production Prachand helicopters for the IAF (10) and army (5), and now the series production will begin. Once the contract for 156 helicopters is signed, HAL will target to execute the order in five to six years.

A fleet of 12 Sukhoi, Sukhoi upgrdes, Space exploration, UAV's, Tejas MK2 and AMCA. The list goes on and on for this monopoly company. We all know we are woefully short of squadron capacity and it is only one company which can fil this by itself and even if India goes for a tender with partners. So what are you waiting for? I am going to fill your quota and kitty with this one. At the height s or depths of its weakness - which is now.

Any moment the engine issue will be solved. Already the Kaveri engine has received a boost due to the delay. Already there are talks of co-development with Safran or Rolls. If Trump who is no Biden decides to pull up GE then this moment of a low PE HAL stock will vanish before you can react. And you have to deal with a high PE Hal stock!!

Designed, developed and extensively test-flown for over a decade by Hindustan Aeronautics Ltd (HAL), the multi-role attack helicopter has been customised as per the requirements of the Indian armed forces to operate both in desert terrains and high-altitude sectors. The LCH is the only attack helicopter in the world that can land and take off at an altitude of 5,000 metres (16,400 ft), which makes it ideal to operate in the high altitude areas of the Siachen glacier. It is also capable of firing a range of air-to-ground and air-to-air missiles and can destroy air defence operations of the enemy.

Even if a private partner like L and T is roped in, it will only add to HAL stock price since deliveries and consequently profit on books will be speeded up. The day the engine issue is solved (which will and which has to happen) that day HAL will be the number 1 stock in the entire worls. Coz no other comapany wil have such pending orders and pent up demand : Tejas MK1, MK1A, MK2, AMCA, UAV and potential exports. Take a breath.

Price: Rs.3060

Solar Industries

- Solar Industries is an Indian company that manufactures industrial explosives and defense products.
- The company's defense segment is its fastest growing segment.
- The company has received orders for the supply of defense products that has double its order book
- The company's order pipeline includes large orders like Pinaka rockets, munitions, and UAVs.
- The company is qualified for Advance Pinaka. Pinaka is on the move.

Solar Industries Ltd (SIL) : A global manufacturer of explosives. SIL's wholly-owned subsidiary EEL for the supply of Area Denial Munition and High Explosive Pre-Fragmented (HEPF) Enhanced rockets. These munitions will be used with the PINAKA Multiple Launcher Rocket System (MLRS), EEL has also been nominated by DRDO as the production agency for all Pinaka Rocket System variations. This Rs 6,084 crore awarded by the Ministry of Defence representing the largest contract in Solar Group's history. 86% of the contract is to be executed within 10 years, with the full timeframe spanning 8 to 15 years.

It also did a deal to establish a major defence and aerospace project in Maharashtra. The agreement, finalized in Davos involves an investment of Rs 12,700 crore. The project aims to expand the production of existing defence products like drones and counter-drone systems, while also introducing new lines such as military transport aircraft. In addition, Solar Industries has also secured export orders of Rs. 2,039 crore with a project duration over the next four years.

So in a short span of couple weeks Solar industries doubled its Order book right in front of your eyes.

Stock: Yearly High of Rs. 13300

Now available at Rs.8660

Another exciting defense star with proven capability and enhancing expanding projects. I find this an attractive stock at this valuation for the next phase of high growth with orders in hand to justify its hype.

Nibe limited

Nibe Ltd in manufactures critical components for the defence sector, e-vehicles, and Software Development.

One of its proposed projects is to build and operate a Private Earth Observation Constellation & corresponding ground segment to provide constellation on lease basis, offer images and analytics as a service

- Nibe Defence and Aerospace Ltd is a subsidiary of Nibe Ltd, which specializes in manufacturing defense components.
- Nibe Ltd also has contracts for subsystems in major projects like the Pinaka launcher, MRSAM, and modular bridges

This 250,000 sq. ft. shop floor will produce components for a new generation of Indian weaponry -- Pinaka rocket launchers and medium range surface-to-air missiles (MR-SAMs).

These new weapons systems have been designed by the Defence Research and Development Organisation (DRDO), with large private companies such as the Tata Group, Larsen & Toubro (L&T) and the Kalyani Group as production partners.

Having known its pedigree in projects and partners let's check out its finances.

The company is debt-free. Wow!

In the last financial year, Nibe posted a turnover of Rs. 100 crore while the company is optimistic will likely triple to Rs. 300 crore and further to turnover of Rs 1,000 crore. Unbelievable!!

SIG SAUER, Inc. is excited to announce a joint venture with Nibe Defence and Aerospace Limited to advance small arms and ammunition manufacturing operations in India.

I would keep it in my kitty now for 1 year duration at least

Why do I say 1 year coz I believe in reevaluating the growth in projects and orders vis a vis the orders on hand and future growth. If such hot stocks catch the wind, investors take these to dizzying heights and that's when I prefer to have a relook whether to cash out, partly, fully or continue. So the exponential growth that can happen in these stocks which are now available at a take off stage of 1 year is time enough to meet and exceed our stock monetary targets and I believe I should not exiting at higher PE levels is a cardinal sin in stocks. It takes away the fizz the dizzy returns and the hardwork of catching these young and anazlying them well enough to enter right at the bottom. Exiting somewhere near the top is also a much needed skill that sadly is rare in the markets and has let to many a sad investing story.

Data Patterns: A year high of 3655

Today at Rs 1350 Data patterns another rising company in the pack is available at a great valuation. At an attractive PE particularly it is just waiting to be packed up

Orders in the pipeline Fire control system for BrahMos missile, Avionics for LCA, RWR for fighter aircraft, ELINT for airborne and ground platform, and Radar subsystems.

Strengths radar systems, electronic warfare, and avionics.

Focus

- Developing large-scale products for the Army, Air Force, and Navy

<u>The Shipping Triplets</u>

- Mazagaon dock
- GRSE
- Cochin Shipyards

For me it is MDL hands down. With about 35,000 cr orders in hand and recently being the sole company in the fray for India biggest defence order of proposed Rs. 70000 crore AIP submarine project with Thysen of Germany being the tech partner, MDL wins.

At Rs.2055 its PE is now at a mouth-watering level for me to start adding in SIPS on every market mood dips.

Next in line is Garden Reach. A stable company with enough orders and capacity to execute GRSE at Rs.1200 (3- Mar-2025), is a nice cherry pick.

<u>The Drones</u>

Keep an eye on Idea Forge – Drone

Zen tech –Simulation and Anti-Drone

Right now the drones are looking like flubby. But believe me, these two can fire up your portfolio. Just waiting for the spark - the drone age is yet to begin. But it will come.

All the above stocks are now available at a better PE value on 3- Mar-2025

For me AMS is the top stock- I believe its stock price will have an absolute scorching trajectory. Followed by HAL and Mazagaon Dock.

BEL gives me stability in stock price movement, dividend and growth.

Nibe, Data patterns, and Solar industries are in the mix definitely.

Idea forge, GRSE and Zen tech are great if they win orders.

<u>That is my portfolio for 2025-26.</u>

Oh. Before I forget I will be in gold futures as much as I can: Watch 19 Mar 2025 For a big spike in gold. (Always few days before and after)

And note I believe is profit booking. Coz I know the year 2025 is full of twists and turns and crashes. And I know the possible dates.

Fundamental Always Wins.
Fundamental: Quality of products plus Orders on Hand.
: A growth trajectory

I stay with the above two simple parameters: Orders and Growth. The external environment whether consumption or military or economic growth. Now the coming two years I would place the external environment as Military.

Prachand
HAL is facing flak including for its quality issues. But here is an example of what it can acheive.

If you think Apache is world class. Then Prachand outclasses apache in various parameters. HAL is up there amongst the best.

Destroying enemy defences, search and rescue missions and anti-tank operations. A datalink system transmits mission data to mobile platforms and ground stations operating within the network.

The two-seater craft also has a tricycle crash proof wheel landing gear and stealth capabilities.

It has extensive flight since it had its first flight 15 years back. The helicopter can fly in high-altitude areas and precisely strike targets at high altitudes. Additionally, it can conduct high-altitude bunker-busting operations

It is the only attack helicopter in the world that can land and take off at height of 5 km and a ceiling of 21 km which again is the highest altitude.

It is also equipped with Forges built FZ231 rocket launcher capable of carrying 70mm rockets, in addition to MBDA air-to-air, air-to-surface and anti-radiation missiles, and Helina anti-tank guided missiles.

Explosive ordinance includes iron bombs, cluster bombs and grenade launchers.

Cockpit

The LCH has a glass cockpit for two crew one behind the other. The cockpit has multifunction displays, target acquisition and designation systems, and a digital video recorder, to capture footage of the battlefield for use in debriefing. A helmet-mounted target system controls the turret guns mounted on the helicopter's fuselage.

Sensors and countermeasures

A charge-coupled device camera, a forward-looking infra-red camera and a laser designator. The two cameras capture the location and position of enemies, ensuring clear visibility during bad weather conditions. The laser range finder and designator aim laser-guided bombs and missiles towards the target.

Radar and laser warning receivers, a missile approach warning system, countermeasure dispensing systems and a missile jammer.

Integrated dynamic system, an anti-resonance isolation system and an integrated architecture and display system.

Engine exhaust Infra-Red Suppression Systems (IRSS).

The IRSS enhances the resilience of aircraft against IR-guided missiles by diminishing the missile lock-on distance and facilitating the superior functioning of IR jammers and flares. A low-backpressure ejector alongside an film-cooled tailpipe, provides defence against both legacy and advanced heat-seeking man-portable air-defence systems.

HAL/Turbomeca Shakti turboshaft engines, each of which can generate 871kW and can run for up to 3,000 hours without maintenance.

You already knew Tejas was awesome. Now you know Prachand is too.

SIX

END GAME

April 14 2025: The defence stocks will take off.

After reading Astro talk and the prospect of coming wars, defence stocks should be high on the list through 2026.

Mar to May 2025: Air plane issues/Terrorists attack

Mar to May 2025: Saturn Conjunct Rahu (in 1968 Assassination of JFK)

Mar 14: 29 deg of Acquarius /Leo : Six month period. Mar- Sep Effects.

Neptune in Pisces with all these: Spiritual groups. Rahu magnifies. Cults in the news.

Neptune rules oil. Oil will make news. Oil spills. Offshore oil rigs. Oil in water news.

Mar 29: Solar Eclipse: Pisces and Virgo Axis: Mercury Venus Neptune, Rahu. Saturn comes in after some time.

Pisces: Denotes Losses, Spiritual, Water

Virgo: Denotes Debates, Perfection, Earth Sign.

Water sign is heavily activated and activates Earth sign with Ketu effect (dissatisfaction, detachment, sword in hand to detach you from your attachment)

Jup in Taurus: Economy

Mars in Gemini: Terrorist, Bomb blast, insurgency (Headless activity due t0 Ketu in Mars), Earthquakes.

Why are so many Planets giving energy to Ketu? Some kind of divine force to start large scale destruction which later brings good? I dont know. But these people are predicting tsunami etc. End of one karmic cycle is the last sign of Pisces. Beginning of a new one after a round of cleansing.

War in Middle East: Iran Saudi, Syria vs West: Major War in 2026.

India can see Earthquakes in South East, youth protests, farmers protest.

Jammu, Himachal, Punjab, Rajasthan. Pakistan, Afghan: water element elevated. Floods or Water related disease in North West India. Indian military can come into action in NW regions of India.

In the World: Naval Wars.

Mar 29 – Saturn transits into Pisces. Solar Eclipse and Amavasya. Water Element is Heavily Activated.

Iran. Middle East: Here we go again.

6 planets in Pisces aspecting Ketu: Happens once in thousand years. Wrong decision from government.

Post 29 Mar: Drastic Change in the World. China will make big moves.

Large Scale downfall in Stocks due to global events post Mar 29.

6 Planets in Pisces: Mar plus Apr 2025. Boom!

30 March: Moon also enters Pisces. Saturn Moves In.

Finishing off karma. Specially Pisces, Aries.

New Beginning.

Ex: If you want to buy a house during this time. That house can become a driver of a next series of events for a lifetime. So any small thing seemingly can become a pivot for a next series of events that can affect your life direction.

Coz of these 6 planets all zodiacs are getting affected. Some more. Some less.

Be careful who you follow, what you see, what you think.

Donate. Spread positive thought and words.

Libra, Aries and Leo: Be careful.

Technology Innovation Modifying Humanity. Evtols, Robots in Medicine. Quantum computing revolution.

Spiritually wonderful Time. Bhadrapadas are active – material life ends. Take a step and thought into spirituality. Do. Donate. Pray.

Rahu: Cheats. Mystery. Illusion. Do not take big loans during Mar- May. Be clear of your objectives.

Education, AI, Robotic, Manufacturing: Expect innovation.

Any restrictions and challenges you need to analyse and learn. So either you improve and win. Or without right effort lose to the competitor.

Mar - Sep: High Drama in the world and In your Life.

North West and South East India: High Effect

Mar – Apr: Artists, Creativity, Researchers, Spiritual, Ai, technology. Good for you all.

Rahu in Aquarius: New beginning. Hello. Look ahead. This is the energy of 2025.

Karma getting over. New one is in your hands to create. With a shot at Moksha thrown in. You Decide. God has given you a choice.

In Mar- Apr 2025.

Play the game of life again. Rahu is there to give the initial chaotic energy.

Or

Take that step towards the other side Like Mahavira. Ketu the headless is ready to detach you.

This Mar-Apr 2025

Decide.

2026: Another story and another book